Advance Praise for
WE WHO DESIRE

Did you ever hear the creative command, *Use your imagination, or someone else will use it for you?* Sue Swartz has used a brilliant, fortified, playful, serious, humanely furious moral imagination, and a poet's love of the music of language, to re-tell the saga of the Bible you thought you knew—and make its implications crystal clear for the life you are right now living. Amen.

—**Alicia Ostriker**, author, *For the Love of God: The Bible as an Open Book*

Consistently on key, Swartz's lyrical voice moves deftly between the Biblical past and our gritty, contemporary moment—often interweaving the two in surprising ways.

—**Yehoshua November**, author, *God's Optimism*

Sue Swartz does magnificent acrobatics with the Torah in WE WHO DESIRE. She takes the English that's become staid and boring, and adds something that's new and strange and exciting. These are poems that leave a taste in your mouth, and you walk away from them thinking, what did I just read? Oh, yeah. It's the Bible.

—**Matthue Roth**, author, *Yom Kippur A Go-Go, Never Mind the Goldbergs, My First Kafka*

It is more than their accessibility that marks Sue Swartz's poems as special—it is the access they give the reader to sudden emotion: wonder, desire, laughter, hurt. Swartz has taken the well-worn motif of Torah commentary-in-verse and created something entirely new and entirely wonderful.

—**Lawrence Bush**, editor, *Jewish Currents*, author, *American Torah Toons, Waiting for God: The Spiritual Explorations of a Reluctant Atheist*

we who desire

Poems and Torah riffs

Sue Swartz

Ben Yehuda Press
Teaneck, New Jersey

Published by Ben Yehuda Press
122 Ayers Court Suite 1B
Teaneck, NJ 07666

http://www.BenYehudaPress.com

Ben Yehuda Press books may be purchased for educational, business, or sales promotional use. For information, please contact:
Special Markets, Ben Yehuda Press,
122 Ayers Court Suite 1B, Teaneck, NJ 07666
markets@BenYehudaPress.com

ISBN13 978-1-934730-51-5

Cover: Detail of "Binary #1" by Sue Swartz

19 18 17 16 / 10 9 8 7 6 5 4 3 2   20160502

In memory:

Anne and Jerry Swartz

Contents

This is the Instruction—

turn it & turn it // leave nothing out
the fire and the splendor
the fire   and the splendor

murmur and sigh
held in each white space

veiled prism of desire

your flesh and blood

Sue Swartz

BEGINNING

Sue Swartz

CREATION

Like a pencil poised for calculation, a key not yet turned
in the twitchy ignition, so was the curved throat of God
in the nothing before the ready,
> so ready, beginning.

Then: Big Bang. Black letters proclaimed onto white
parchment universe—

Water swirling away from water. Sapphire sky
pouring through. Crackling horizon, pulsing light—

Seeds sprouting into fruit, into trees ripe with the will-be—

Whirling serpents and creepers of the soil; swarming,
leaping, winged things—

And last to come, dusty youngsters made in the image
> (haploid or diploid, twin & twin)—

Each particle & personality called into itself by a word.

A voice. Insistent, unfurling. The deafening pulse
of now:
> so good.

(this and that God created us)

& God said:
I will bring before you every living thing of the field
plus every fowl of the heavens and you, you will call out its name.

& the Human said: Chicken.
    Heifer, giraffe, osprey. Chipmunk, boa
    constrictor, saddle-horse, dog—

& thus continued to name each thing in its turn, all the naked,
yelping array of creation. And the Human said:
    This is very, very good.

(And it was a new day.)

And after a while, the Human went out from the land of pleasure
into thorn and sting-shrub, to painful labor of all kinds.

& the Human continued to name:
    Betrayal, mine, forbidden, kin. Finite. Desperation.

& all the lesser things of the earth:
    Kike, kaffir, nigger, rag head. Fag, wetback, redneck, goy—

Such a simple little game.

❧

We lived in each other's flesh then, shared lungs and heart,
bone & sinew. There was no inside, no outside; no cold, no hunger.

It was paradise. Tired at day's end we slept, cradled by familiar
mulch, dreamt our honeyed dreams. The ground tilted, shrouding
us with the pull of something more—

Sue Swartz

You will be.

Enticing: You will be. Gasping, grasping, I reached for the unseen.
He woke first, saw me motionless—
        Shouts punched the air.

       Bone from my bones! Flesh from my flesh!
       She will be called woman for she comes from me.

My limbs – *my* limbs – shuddered. I rose, shivering at sudden
exposure, walked out from the canopy of green. I would not have
named him such if he had been lying there,
                      struggling toward—

❧

She's come undone.
She didn't know
what she was headed for,
and when I found what she was headed for,
it was too late.

Reaching. Biting into. Purposeful un-becoming.

Creator, shall I bloom?

This is how it begins.

❧

And this is how it goes on.

The first child created by humans: miracle.
A second born: he goes by the name *mortal.*

Only one can be favored.

Then: arm raised with the intention of.
Then: blood-shock exile.

This is the book of begettings.

Page after page come the generations,
bruising & mourning, striving and striding.

Begetting and begetting in the likeness of.

    (Seth. Lamech. Enosh.

    Another.

    Another. Another.
    Another. Another.)

The thrum of humans is great upon the Earth.

In every generation we hold the rock—
    (tire iron   electrode
    to the groin
    knife small enough
    to be stashed in a shoe.)

In every generation God reconsiders,
    regrets anew.

MNEMONICS

On that day all the fountains of the great deep burst apart—

Three-alarm. Tsunami. Midnight knock on the door.
It is unclear when – but not if – the great deep
will make its will known. Sixty seconds or a length of days—

No matter. The once firm ground has already
begun to drift. Will you grab that photo of your father
at his work bench, pleasure of joinery unmistakable?

Or will it be the silver candelabra, a tender note from your ex?

Noah had the animals two-by-two, every rump and mewling
a bookmark for where he left off. And though God's prompts
(glorious rainbow, bit of flesh) are meant to span eons, all memory
is insufficient: a capricious ill-fitting device so unlike the dove
in her graceful out

& back, out and back.

Forget the strike-anywhere matches, the sack of flour.

Stuff your bag with impractical things: rose and sketch,
locket and shell, all those landmarks of where you've been.
It's easy to forget what brought you to this flooded place.
As the world bursts apart, place your hand on that—

Remember to ask forgiveness of all you left behind.

(and its name was called Babel)

After the drenching and after the dove—

With everything a freaking mess, a junkyard horizon
(tin cup & steel girder, dog-less collar & moldy scarf)—

With far too many gone missing, gone quiet, crazy
tired, and overwhelmed by the muck—

With 72 voices in your head, each equally cajoling—

    (Could you be a bit more specific—

    Oh, hell, I can't understand a word you're—)

Who wouldn't speak a ziggurat up to heaven,
a towering lexicon of blame?

☿

After the collapse of best laid plans,
your head in the clouds, the rest of you mid-fall—

Trying not to be brought low by the din
of so many beginnings, wishing for a verse of advice.

Here: Plant a vineyard. Here: Get a little drunk.

Speak a new language into the soggy world.
Stash that box of nails and hold onto your hat.

Yes, the scaffolding shakes from time to time
when the sky is howling, and even when it's still.

Sue Swartz

ENTROPY / FAITH

Abraham: Go forth from your native land and from your
father's house to the land I will show you.

We are nothing at first. Little more than dust, lucid
with possibility—
    Then fruit flies and feral dogs on our way
to becoming a different kind of multitude.

Go forth, we are commanded, and one by one we go
careening into an arrangement we barely understand,
leave our ancestral home to make our way, strangers
parading about in fancy suits of flesh.

We sacrifice our choicest herds, mark the bodies
of our young, yet nothing seems to make us right.
Like a bird we crash into windows.

Like an inflamed god we destroy our things.

To be fair, there is naiveté on every side. The first law
of the universe goes like this—
    Energy neither comes nor goes, just whirls
about, fools us into believing there's something new
under the sun.

The second? Live long enough in the closed system
of a promise and things will go wrong.

Stars will fall off the edge, solar plexus flicker,
kneecap spin off wildly. This is the truth the dead know:
    The meat on our bones is dodge & ruse,
    short-lived show to tempt our acceptance.

And we do again and again, sign on the dotted line.

Even as eternity rights itself & the skin of our lives
fails to outlast time. Still we invoke the third law, the favored,
the one we call perfection.

Sue Swartz

(catastrophe)

Shall I mention to Abraham what I am about to do?

Pity the angels their impossible task—

Having to say:
> Leave the city, your only one, the one that you love,
> with its taxi stops and north wind, butcher shops
> and wash hanging on the line.

Having to say:
> Take hold of your sons & daughters, your reluctant
> spouse.

Having to be believed.

There's no escaping it. Each of us may be called on
at any moment to serve this way, messenger for a message
we're unsure of.

See, behind you, a phone dangling off the hook, glass jar
tipped open on its side.

Wild boars roam freely, lapping salt wherever they find it.

The sky is crimson, the stench of bodies floods the soft
earth, but here we remain in the midst of our 10-fold
bargaining, the last to see what is already foreseen.

Surely God in heaven could have come in person to advise.
>   (*Don't look*—)

Pity the message its compulsion to be heard, its bone
white lament:
> Why do you set yourself against me?

And he (Abraham) sent her (Hagar) away.

Perhaps she heard it wrong—

No way will she and the boy be thrust out, not now,
not this soon, with only some bread & a skin of water.

Perhaps she stretches out her hand:
    Will you really deliver us to the barren desert?

Or intones his name over and over, sobbing
like the last woman on Earth.

Pity the story its need to move forward:
    Its devotion to conclusion, the ruthless pace
    of anguish.

See the small tribe of man woman boy enacting
a present etched in black fire.

Imagine the dialogue within—

    (No.) (No.) (No.)

Take your son, your favored one...

Pity survivors their providence—

Having to say:
    Once I had faith servitude would serve me.

Having to say:
    Once I gathered up firestone and twig gladly,

Sue Swartz

but what has come to pass has caught me
up short.

Having to look back.

Each of us may be called upon. See behind you—

A boy, mute, favored son of a jealous mother.
Some wood. Ram roasting on a spit.

The story enters without mercy. Surely God in heaven
could have come in person to say.
        (*One can live without having survived—*)

Pity. Pity all around.

ELEGY

His sons Isaac and Ishmael buried him—

Everything begot then begets its opposite:
nothing stays itself for very long.

It was time for Abraham to go, and for his sons—

One sent out, hand pressed firmly on his back,
one led forward by deception luminous as the stars—

To bury him.

Oh, to be a fly on the wall at Machpelah as the grand
patriarch is laid within.

Tell me. Which son would speak first of his restless
consolations?

Which of his many little deaths?

(with reference to our conflicting desires)

Isaac pleaded on behalf of his wife—
Rebecca conceived, but the children struggled in her womb—

Let us claim our curiosity, we who have sisters and brothers
of an altogether separate flesh. Though we no longer steal glimpses
in a circus sideshow, still we look, drawn in by the tangled blood
vessels, centimeters shared by neighboring skulls, skin that will not
allow the two to walk away. Also by their fierce desire to see the
other face to face.

Here, the sisters in shared black headscarf. Here, smiling in scrubs
before the operation. Courageous! *Beautiful!*

We cheer them on, refusing to admit contingency below. Laleh's
blood could not sustain itself. Ladan died 90 minutes later—
     More like us than they could know. By us I mean the rest
of us, those who praise separation, but spend a lifetime seeking the
truest twin, an intimate so close as to be indistinguishable, close
enough to share vein and bone.

In the beginning we are alone in the night of our mother's body.
Despite the shared slice of code, the bits of blood, there is always
the same sorry ending—
     We are sent out, grasping and rough-hewn, past the four
rivers, past the nameless animals and fruit-laden trees, past the
winged cherubim with their blazing swords, into the living.

Return? Not possible. And worse yet – will she love us as we are?

By us, I mean those who scrutinize their solitary skeletons for what
they lack, even as they steal their sibling's birthright. Those able to
roll side to side carelessly during sleep, careen downhill on bikes.

Dr. Kenneth Goh, siding with the sisters, said *You're the guy holding the knife, so you better know what you're doing.* I give him credit—
        To cut through bone knitted together like ivy, to try
with godly chutzpah to right the faulty promise given one mother,
that deep in her wriggling womb, a being is taking shape, one nation
created in her image, heralding the future.

To pick up Solomon's knife. In the end, of course, none of it is fair.
The yearning, the choice, the cutting. And worse yet—
        Will no one ever understand us?

By us I mean all of us. With our desire to see the other face to face.
With our desperate need to walk away.

(Isaac's eyes were dimmed)

And Rebekah instructed Jacob to put on his brother's skins—

Are you really my son Esau?

How willing we are to believe
the other of what is.

Is there no blessing for me too, Father?

There is no absence
that cannot be replaced.

SLEEP ON A BED OF STONES

(Jacob) slept on a bed of stones and dreamt of angels—

The deadliest season since climbing began, storms
claiming twelve with sudden vengeance. Frozen bodies
are left on the slopes, human cairns teasing the next
expedition and the next.

Sherpa or American, nationality means nothing
at twenty-seven, eight, nine thousand feet where limbs
twist in on themselves from air tenuous as love.

Everything is foreseen, though free will is given—

You quote me Akiva when I insist no one
has any business on that slickness of mountain,
skating the unbounded ice fields—

And gift me a box, small and unadorned by ribbon
or bow, the avalanche of angles a delight
to your mathematician's eye. White on white borders
bleed one into the other, perfect cube marked only
by the space it is not.

        I turn the box in my hand,
feel for the intersection where one edge begins
and another ends.

Perhaps it isn't madness that propels us to approach
the clouds, wings spread wide, but desire—

To transform hard corners into soft & slippery planes,
just as air whooshed into a cube will spill its secrets
onto the jagged horizon, white against dazzling color,
white against white against white.

ANATOMY OF THE THIGH

And Jacob wrestled with the angel until dawn—

What does the human thigh know?

Muscle, fascia, and blood, inguinal ligament,
saphenous vein; stretch of plié, ache
for the lover's caress.

It should not, is not
meant to know
the sear of flaming gasoline
tendons ripped apart by wire
or common nails blown deep into the tenderness
of a young woman, nails
which in another time might be used
for the floorboards of a new start,
her leg which in another time
might feel the brush of flimsy skirt,
her name exploded into history
on the Number 18
Egged bus.

If the thigh asked for a bite of our shining apple,
would we comply, knowing
that after the first burst of red
our wild-eyed romance with death
would be laid bare?

How could we stand to say:
      You who were innocent at dawn
      shall be no more.

How could we stand to say:
      This shambling sorrow, too,
      is a blessing.

(the book of women)

And Leah birthed—
And Rachel was barren—

This is the book of women—

In it, the body's fruit is legal tender.
In it, sons are made in the image of stranger,
master, lover, king.

Status is earned between the thighs.

Also, this is the book of virile possessions
       (flocks
       servants
       wives).

And the book of volatile love.
In it, put out and put up with.

In it, sisterly deception and desperate measures.
       All those mandrakes!
       All those fancy push-up bras!

❦

And Dinah went out... (and) Shechem lay with her by force—
Then he spoke to the maiden tenderly.

In it, gathering flowers in broad daylight.
In it: parking lot, backyard, Tuesday night date.

Where brother, stranger, husband.
Where alcohol, opportunity, tithe of war.

Also, this is the book of he said, she said.

Sue Swartz

And the book of failure to report.
   None of it happened.
   Or maybe every last detail.

In it, men hold on to what is theirs.
Force and tenderness is found on every page.

Read between the lines—
   There's a woman telling her story.

❦

   Jacob lifted his eyes and saw Esau coming,
   and with him 400 men.

When pleasure is spoken of in past tense—
When your selves do not add up—
Your wife calls you by another name—
Your brother loves you after all—
When your babies grow into women you cannot corral,
   men with steel in their hands—
When more has been taken than you have left—
You have arrived at the nub of your story.

❦

virility duplicity
all that comes to pass

everything begot
begets its opposite

message you cannot elude
gifts you cannot parse

all you are
in relation to the other

Rachel died and was buried on the road.

This is the book of sorrow.

In it, Rachel weeping for her children.
It in, grief plentiful as stars in the sky.

In it, the 14-year-old girl who—
The boy sitting next to her when—

All that is born from the body's fruit,
wrestling with what names us.

Ceasing to be coming to be.

WHAT THE DAY CANNOT CONTAIN

Joseph dreamt a dream and told it to his brothers—

A woman for sale buys herself back.

Flesh adheres to bone, growing old, growing strong.
Nothing crumbles from neglect.

Bulldozers sit idle for lack of direction.

The pin refuses to leave the grenade, the machete
refuses the portal of bloody earth.

Soap is free of charge, also vitamins, also incense
and the roof does not cave in from this freedom.

Lovers stop keeping accounts.

The spark of revenge goes damp in our throats.

A man pulls a thread out of his glittering coat
and weaves it through our long-abandoned wanting.

We sway like sheaves of wheat at harvest.

Enemies lay down their rusty shovels, all distance
reconciled.

A pit offers up grape clusters and hyacinth.
Charred wood and scrap metal offer up a new city.

The city finds a heart in its thickening walls,
the heart finds time to set free its grief.

Thus does the night embrace the dreamer.
Open your mouth like a motherless child.

(appetite)

And they pitched him in a pit without water and sat down
to eat bread—

Sometimes we are Joseph of the ornamented coat, all grand notion
and provocation. Sometimes we are the brothers, punch-drunk
on all we're not. Sometimes we are the yawning pit at twilight,
sometimes the water, sometimes the bread.

❧

The body longs—

When the stomach growls, we search for food, hold out our pitchers
for a downpour—
                    And also it consents.

Forget fried chicken and truffles. Forget popcorn and mascarpone.
If hungry enough, we will gorge on rancid tomatoes, wash down
our cravings with lye. We will certainly swallow lies, confuse day
with night, sell what is not ours for a taste of happiness.

Sit with me a while at this table.

❧

There is the dream of bread
        and there is the dream of pistachio and honey.

There is the dream of the unlocked door
        and there is the dream of arriving, arrival.

There is the dream of peaceable borders,
        the dream of soft linen and polished silver.

Sue Swartz

There is the dream of split-level houses
and the dream of *on the cover of the Rolling Stone.*

There is the dream of those who came before
        and the dream they could never imagine—

The dream of forgetting,
        the dream of becoming, the dream of belonging—

The dream of home
        which is not home, which is not yet home.

🌰

        I am Joseph your brother whom you sold into Egypt—

Envy the sons of Leah their rare fortune—

To see Joseph in all his awesome splendor,
their terrible fling with fate unfolding
in undreamed-of ways, their brother hero, broker,
sandaled powerhouse of all Egypt.

There is a moment we are sure it will happen,
when Joseph will raise his sceptered hand
and ragged misery will overflow its flimsy purse.

Yet no exilic punishment awaits the brothers,
no waterless pit. Just the narrows of guilt split open
like ripened figs.

He's letting them off easy! They're getting away with it!

The spark of revenge has gone damp. But really,
it's like this—
        If I were an orphan, I'd bow down
        before anyone with news of home.

If I were lonely, I'd grind my grievances
fine as sand and feast.

❦

*Jacob's entire household went down into Egypt
because there was no bread—*

And *Homo Erectus* out of Africa,
out of the Levant, out of everywhere known—

Across the Pacific on a highway of kelp.
Tracking mammoth through the Bering Straits—

From Mississippi when boll weevil and killing floods—

Through tunnels & sagebrush,
house to house in the freedom night—

From Belarus to Dimona, Miami on a wooden boat—

Ebudae into Khartoum, across the border in a pick-
up truck. When gold dust & open harbors—

From Petra to Basra, Aqaba
to Indus with cardamom and silk—

From the Texas Panhandle when poverty & dust—

When potatoes ran out. When kidnappers & kings—

When something unimagined.
When something unsayable.

When reconciliation and the deafening pulse—

Called to ourselves, we went in search of.

Sue Swartz

Sue Swartz

CROSSING

Sue Swartz

NAMELESS

The Egyptians set taskmasters over them—

They built garrison cities.

> *(And I would carry water. And I would sweep—)*
> *(And I would weave with wool, with rope—)*
> *(And I would check the fishing nets at dawn—)*

And when their fingers bled—
> *(My owner would dip them in oil*
> *and light a match to them.)*

And they stayed because they didn't have anywhere to go.
And they stayed because they were animals, property.

> *(And they would beat me. They would whip me.)*

And they stayed because—

> *(She whipped me with a whip and opened my skin*
> *so then I never—)*

This is the book of not-seeing.
    This is the book of what we allow.

(what is held within)

And their lives were embittered—

I lift the sweater over my head
and its name tumbles out across my winter skin—
favorite— just like the names stored up inside me
        (*daughter, poet, human*)
that tumble out whenever they will.

Every everything ends up this way, enfolded
and awaiting release.

No wonder our words are often muddled,
caught between competing tyrannies of what is
and what *really* is, what was and could yet be.

No wonder I cling to the weave,
its soft camaraderie, turn from the narrative within—

> *Night-shift. Fire.*
> *Stampede.*
> *Locks.*
> *Searchlights.*
> *Rubble.*

> *Fabric—*
>   *Ash—*

> *Bone. Hands searching*
> *after their dead.*

There are some stories so intimate, they bind
themselves to you forever. Some namings so precise
        (*complicit*)
you flee them all the days of your life.

I set the sweater aside, my body a repository
of silenced everythings. I did not build
this vault of desolation, but now, *now* I live in it.

I do not wish to serve the fierce taskmaster
of truth, but it towers over me bloody and alive.

(reaching)

Their cry for help from bondage rose up to God—

all day the sun
all day the sun beating
all day hands moving
hands hammering
        shame into brick
hands blistering
submitting
all day, all day the sun
beating down on the bitumen
embittering
coating hands thick
the sun beating
hands building
hands building up
sculpting palaces
fashioning spires
and all day the sun
the sun shaming, hands
reaching
hands forgetting
all day forgetting
        what they were meant for
everything is the sun
all day the beating sun
and hands moving
hands hammering
hungering
bodies bent
burning
despairing—

all day falling
the sound of bodies
    falling softly on sand

bodies of the nameless—
bodies of their children—

of their outstretched lives
God took notice

(i-will-be-sent-me-to-you)

In the flame of a fire out of the midst of a bush—

First memory: the gentle push of water.

What I learned in the palace—
    The ease with which we put up with others'
    suffering.

Yes, judgment overcame me. I struck the overseer
& buried him.
    (We have all held that particular rock.)

Then I ran – which is different than escaping.

And I married – which is different than embracing –
    and tended the flocks in perfect silence.

Slowly I understood, but looked away.
    Not now, I'm busy.

My skin was crackling. I stumbled on my tongue.
    Isn't there some other way?

I threw my sandal, craved the comfort of lesser gods.
    Why me? What if?

I cannot speak, don't want to speak. If I speak,
then this and only this—

Are you what you say?

LIVE YOUR WAY INTO THE ANSWER

Because *against this, that*
Because the angels of our better nature
And the angle of days to come
Because as we said goodbye   As we say goodbye

Because this is the book of bursting through
And the book of coming undone
Because bricks without straw
Because bruise without respite

And the compulsion to be heard
Because the crack in everything
          And because the darkening

Because the darkness
And the daughter of Pharaoh in every generation
Because the distance between
And the dog,
          chained in some fool's backyard: barking and barking—
Because the dream of crossing

Because the ego that dreamt   (its elliptical nature)
And the events of the night—

Because the faceless god of frogs & thunder
And the faithful god of time
Because the fear   And the fire   And the fissure
Because glimpses of—

And Heisenberg's uncertainty

Because *I cannot live on tomorrow's bread*
Because I-will-be sent me to you
Because if this, then that   And imagine all the people

And in the interstices, hidden

Because joining one thing to another
Because knee deep in muddy water
Because the light of a candle
        in the heart of the sun

Because locusts & lice   And the long strange trip
Because love supreme   And the luminous underneath

Because mantles marked   Because metaphoric
Meteoric   And the middle that will not hold

Because naked ambition   And nothing as it was
And the one who takes off her shoes

And the one and the one and the one—

Because of this *permeable world*

And the photo that spreads beyond the frame
Because the point of no return   And the portable palace
Because the protests in Tahrir Square
        (All that purposeful unbecoming)

Because the quotidian
Because the radical

Because the sea filled with baskets
And seeing an angel in the marble, he carved
Because starry, starry night   And a steel bar can be bent

Because suitcases filled with suffering
Because the touchable—

Because the unleavened—   And the vertical drop.

Because what is in your hand
And what I am is what I am   And when you drew the map
And where we're going, there's no—

Because who will live in our house
And who will memorize our story
And why we're whispering   Why we're whispering
                as we say goodbye

Because xenophobia
Because you and you and you
Because zealotry and zeitgeist

And the Zen koan: *one drop reveals the ocean*
Because zero & zilch & zip
Because the zany zookeeper
                unlocked the cage—

LIBERATION

Hold out your arm towards the sky and there will be darkness—

Let my people—

blood   frogs   lice   wild animals   pestilence
boils   hail   locust   darkness   slaying

of the first-born—

By each scourge, you will know I am God.

🐛

Let my people—

We were slaves (what if we were never slaves?)
willing to believe in the extraordinary night.

How it must have looked—
        River scarlet, the sky darkening // darkening.

🐛

The line dividing good and evil runs
        through the heart of every human being.

The heart may suffer the line, but the hand suffers the act.

The heart may pooh-pooh its inherent split, but the hand
pauses mid-air, considers whether to push the button.

You must go on—
        Stanley Milgram thus reproached the hesitant
in his experiments.

So did they punish an anonymous unknown with
escalating volts. Despite pounding, despite pleading—

Despite shouts of pain & the silence following, two-
thirds of them gave in.

Later, many would say they were grateful for the fleeting
glimpse of *i* and *I*, the god and God within.

Later, Moses would say—
        I was caught up in the thrill of the moment.

And later the hand—

❦

{God did this for me when I went out. For me.

Of course I followed the rules, smeared my doorpost
with blood. Of course I was spared.

Wouldn't you? Weren't you?}

❦

        Slaying of the firstborn—

Because our fingers bled—
Because they beat us, whipped us—

When the cries went up from Egypt—

Drunk on the night's anthem, I wanted
it, this pummeling.

On the other hand, dreaded messenger,
God's hired gun:
> Why the bleating sheep in pasture?
> Why the children in their beds?

Angel of Death, agent of freedom:
> Why so much blood on my blistered hands?

I am dizzy from such signs and wonders.
Let me go into the grief-soaked night.

❦

> *You shall go free on this day, in the month of Spring—*

all night
all night the cries
all night the edge—
> the edge of freedom
came near
closer
altering // deafening

and all night
the moon
shone high and bright
so bright
it burned to cinder
every question

all night the cries
all night the tears
the gasps

as life broke apart—
theirs and ours—

stopped
      mid-sentence.

✤

      And Pharaoh and his courtiers had a change of heart—

This is the book of going out—
      the brink was un-crossable,
      yet we crossed.

Strange not to be held back, this round-
about unfurling in the dark, bodies arced
around promise (whisper //

wash of smoke)—

      How could we have known
(we who knew nothing but bricks
& sun & the arid // arid flat-lined ground)—

That the calling of the sea is to surround?

Plunged into the deep like a stone—

Wall of water to our right. Wall of water
to our left. For us, a miracle. For *them*—

      Catastrophe. The book of rupture
in the order of things.

How it must have looked, water separated
from water—

Everywhere, story mid-stride.

MANNA

When the Israelites saw it, they said to one another,
"What is it?"

A seed. A wafer. A good sign—
    This hunger.

I want, I want—
      Great is the act of wanting.

Great is the act of eating,
      the act of feasting on fields of dew.

And great is the act of imagining—

That the dew is bread.
      That the bread is something more.

More, there, at the savory margin—

APOLOGIA

The people stood at the foot of the mountain—

We were unbound then // awakened from watery sleep
when the earth cracked open & sound poured out like lava.

We were undecided then // bathed in sulfur and smoke
when thunder split the mountain // when lightening

scorched our heels. Poised on the edge of desire // enveloped
by rumbling flashes, the words entered our consciousness

like a tornado—
        In the bleached-blind wilderness we stood // amid
fire clouds and roaring triumph // amid searing trumpets

& our endless endless wanting // and we were afraid.
Ruthless present tense // Mobius arc of time—

We were joined to each other then // to the blistering
mountain // the vertiginous moment // every noun and verb

exploded through the wilderness. Chosen agnostics,
we declaimed yes to deliverance // yes to unspecified

constraint. To the shattering of silence // to the shattering
of stone. For you not yet able to speak, we said *yes.*

(after the glory)

These are the rules that you shall set before them.

After the glory, the rules.

After the broad vista of miracle, the proximity
of order—
        If this, then that.

If an angry ox gores someone, is its flesh to be eaten?

If a man shoves a pregnant woman, what is the suitable
eye for eye? Bruise for bruise?

What if the eye is that of a slave?
What if the slave shares your likeness of face?

What of the sorceress? What of the dreamer?
And what of the lonely thief caught while breaking in?

This is the book of yet another contingency,
every reader with a different point of view—

        What if the bruises are self-inflicted?
        What if I'm caught while standing on one foot?

❦

If the slave says to her master
        I do not wish to go free

Her ear shall be pierced with an awl, wound
that will not heal, the mark of elusion.

If a man seduces a virgin, he cannot say
     You may go now

He must make good on his promise, set a border
'round his life, be her partner in misery.

❦

Don't wrong a stranger.
Don't overtax the poor.
Don't ill treat the widow or orphan.
No false rumors.
No joining hands with the guilty.
No sorcery, thievery, bestiality.
No other gods besides me.

Divine law is money thrown in a beggar's cup—
     never enough, always too much.

❦

Out we came from a house of slaves.
     (We will do—)

With willing servitude etched on our animal skin.
     (We will listen—)

Freedom is hauling a bucket of live coals.
     (Unasked for. Unpredictable.)

     To put it down is forbidden.

ON THE MOUNTAIN

And God said come up to me—

Forget the wind and the wait.

Forget your shivering.

Here is bonfire etched in stone,
scroll of glowing sapphire.

Whirlpools and radiance.

(explanation after the calf)

It was the sound of battle—
It was the sound of song—

God of human impatience—
God of inhuman desire—

Creator of lost bearings—
       Of cowardice & awkward offering—

Truly, do not be vexed with us.

Yes, we assembled quite illegally,
bestowed our gold rings to the fire.

And yes, we mistook shine & stature
       for your unstructured kiss—

       The work of our hands for creation.

But God of the impossible face—
God of infinite revision—

Do not blame us for the calf,
       for we are a lonely & unpracticed people.

Frightened of the waiting,
       the disappearance of our chains.

Oh God of perfumed mercy—
Creator of temptation & accident & fate—

Reset our bodies to the clock of your demands.

Forgive the plague of our wandering
    attentions—

    All there is to know of love
    we learned from your back.

(place where the future hides)

Carve yourself two tablets of stone like the first ones—

This is the book of vacant lots, the feral space
        between anguish and anguish.

In it: used condoms & broken glass—

Regrets numerous as stars.

In it: fight and flight in a single breath—

        Homage to the cadence of now.

And this is the book of second chances, the sugary
        donut we devour in gratitude.

In it: self-help gurus & teary promises—

Purposeful becoming. Engraving over, beyond.

In it, we become a people—

        To put us down is forbidden.

LET THEM BUILD ME A HOLY PLACE

Fine linen, tanned ram skins, acacia wood and oil for lighting—
And I shall dwell among them—

White lunchboxes. A dangling cigarette. Eleven men mid-air,
thigh to thigh on iron girder held aloft by coiled rope.

I imagine the unnamed photographer shot this precise angle,
welded the men to posterity because of what lies beyond
in the milky haze:
      Spires and tenements, storefronts and docks,
        the unlit marquees & willowy treetops of Central Park.

Yes, that's the hook, the *beyond*—

The floating *out*-there, tumbling *down*-there (the absence
of fear, the assemblage of extraordinary space).

But the real action is above, home of hammer rising
to stamp the border, steel rising to pierce the unmanageable blue.

We're always joining one thing to another, we beings
made in the image. A poem is not a cathedral
     is not a rocket ship,
        not a stone obelisk
           or a tower of steel,
though each is an address for our hunger. Each reminds us
it is the intention of height and not height itself that defines.

That our vision goes farther than our eyes can ever see—
      Right up to the edge of infinite at the center
      of the world.

Sue Swartz

(mutable cloud)

And the building was complete—
And a cloud covered the Tent of Meeting—
And if the cloud was raised, the Israelites would embark
on their journeys—

Who among us hasn't played the game

of naming that which we cannot touch

of supposing fibrous wisp to be torso /

tiger / palace shifting across pure palette

of sky / loneliness or love or pride

called out in thin disguise?

Who among us hasn't held their atlas

close / bounded map of comings and goings

our compulsion to make haste inscribed

in mutable blue on every page?

Who hasn't looked up / looked out

toward elsewhere waiting for a sign?

Sue Swartz

CALLING

Sue Swartz

THE BOOK OF BLOOD AND GUTS

> *He shall lay his hand upon the head of his offering*
> *and slaughter it—*

That first turkey sandwich after my veggie days
went up in smoke—
      Ah, thick sourdough, thrill of mayonnaise.

Animal nature won out, old-time religion: I bit into
the flesh without apology. Pride should keep me
from admitting this (though you can only sacrifice
what costs you)—
      What I noticed was *salt*. The meat needs salt.

Not—
      My meal was once muscle and sinew,
a squawking creature known to open its mouth
in the pouring rain and drown.

Not—
      Underpaid illegals made possible this almost-
perfect moment, 70 80 throats a minute, a blood river
coursing through Memphis & Boonestown...

An entire story of separation.
Forget it. Salt soon gave way to thoughts of a friend
of a friend who—
      Consumed by the rules inside her,
sliced her wrists once, again, and then again until
she was made whole.

Faced with such bare determination, what could
we do? We washed and wrapped her body,
scattered her ashes. Scattered her, and walked away.

If you're going to do a thing, do it right—
      This is what came to me, the once-alive
held firmly in my hands. Come right up against it.

Friends, *Leviticus* is not for children, though they may
find its slime and innards irresistible. This book is for us,
the fully-grown & loosely tethered—
      Priests of limitation, doyens of pain.

(sacrifice)

1.   *Ola* (Ascent-offering)

We built a chimney—
Suet, plumage, innards, smoke
feed our hungry god.

2.   *Mincha* (Near-offering)

Lungs resin-thick—let
us share sweet cakes, thighs touching,
as flames kiss us close.

3.   *Shalom* (Gift-offering)

A sacred greeting—
Small bodies passed into death.
Ash rises in praise.

4.   *Hattat* (Sin-offering)

Our lonely failures—
dirty insides, tainted meat—
licked clean by the blade.

5.   *Asham* (Guilt-offering)

Lamb, goat, turtledove.
We did not mean to do it:
kill and kill and kill—

ON THE EIGHTH DAY

> *Aaron's sons Nadav & Avihu... offered before God*
> *strange fire that had not been commanded—*

On the eighth day, Alessandro Volta
put metal coins on his tongue
and prophesied sulfurous electricity.

On the eighth day, Leucippus
considered the true nature of the void,
Teller the true capacity of the sun.

Curie was entranced by radium,
and Maxwell by luminous radiations.

On the eighth day, there were isotopes,
cloud chambers, alpha rays.

Life was vaporized in a simple test of hydrogen.

On that day outside planned creation,
God peered into the universe and was afraid for us—

Noisy children snapping berries
off a poisonous bush, racing down the street
with pointy twigs—

> *Didn't I tell you to knock that off?*

And burned to the nub two sons of priestly
inheritance. Before the whole assembly
were they offered up, a soothing savor.

Object lesson: *this* may you burn
in your copper pan, of this sinew and thigh

may you eat.

But this intoxicating notion, *this* 4-legged
swarming-thing—
        It is polluted meat. Strange fire.

Your blowtorch future.

CLEAN

And the following shall make you tamei—

<u>In the birthing-tent</u>

> *A woman, when she produces-seed and bears…*
> *(she) remains unclean for seven days—*

When a woman sprouts like Eve, carries her bellyful
of precious cargo proudly around town, caution her—

(Though she will slip into true belief the moment:

How wondrous the eyelids and wisp of hair! The tiny
mouth and whimpering hunger!)

Tell her—

This is the book of fevers. In it, men in stiffened
frock coats, their hands fresh-splattered from autopsy.

In it, Mary Shelley binds her creature to this world.
Something wild passes close. Feel it—

Water swirling away from water, creation's aperture open—
> *The heartbeat on its little wheels!*

❧

<u>Disease theory</u>

> *When a person has a swelling, rash, or shiny spot,*
> *(he) is to be brought to Aaron the priest—*

How we labor to contain the body's disruptions.

As a child, I imagined miniature men inside me
pulling miniature levers, turning miniature dials.

Sore throat or stomachache, they were to blame,
ill-tempered technocrats in their little black suits.

What did I know of sewer gas or night air?
Pharmacology & rare anatomies of the blood?

I knew nothing. When Dr. Wagner said, "Open
up," I opened. When he said, "swallow this," I did.
Miscellaneous fever, bruising, and ooze—
my parents trusted his ability to lift the curse.

What did they know of my strange company,
how together we formed the perfect whole?

❦

Diagnosis

> When the priest looks at him and here.... (A) man with tzara'at,
> he is unclean, yes, "Unclean! Unclean!" shall the priest declare
> him—

Damn. Another 3 a.m. flying dream. This time I'm on a cement slab
hurtling toward overgrown lawns covered with large plastic pigs

& spiked coat hangers. This is not what normal people dream.
Awake, I tilt on a giant seesaw of guilt by association and realize:

I might not know what normal is. My dead left many clues,
not one legible note of instruction for navigating this crossroad.

Minds taken in by spirals and whirligigs, Greek letters & the price of toilet paper, they wore the warp & woof of affliction stoically.

Seamlessly, one might say, and with understated finesse. Running off to Florida on a manic whim, electrodes for breakfast. Washing.

Washing, washing, again, again, again. Garments torn & heads made bare, they bob in and out of traffic, sit sorting, counting.

My dead have secrets. That much is abundantly clear. I listen for whispers of their generous madness, find they've come

while I'm asleep. Bad timing is all I've got, and fingerprints left on the towels. Of course I don't shush them away— then I'd lose

the true nature of everything. I claim my kin, their fleshy wisdom. How else to name my own impurities and small derangements?

❦

Radioactivity

> *The priest is to enter and when he looks, and here—*
> *Tzara'at has spread in the house, it is acute affliction in the*
> *house, it is unclean—*

> *"Power Company Buys Ohio River Village*
> *Plagued by Clouds of Acid."*

Once the walls
    of the house were newborn. They hungered
    for the trespass of picture hooks, shriek of accidental crayon.

The walls
    are humbled by time. Three coats of China White
    cover fingerprint and love-sickness, all the slender clichés
    of daily living.

Sue Swartz

The walls
>of the house are sulfur-woozy. They sputter and cough blue
>down to the studs.

The priests
>of examination have examined. The priests of litigation
>have litigated. All declare Unclean! Unclean!

Thus are the walls
>without prospect, swaying trees marked in red. Gray house,
>white house, bottle green. Beige.

Next door
>and next door, next door and next, the walls of the town
>will soon be gone.

Machines will roar—

>*And a spalling of plaster; complete destruction,* stones
>and timber undone in the un-building.

❧

How we measure oblivion—

60 kilograms. 43 seconds. Landscape blasted flat.

Gargantuan steel ruins, splayed open like peaches.
Silhouettes seared into anything that will hold.

Creation's aperture closed.

BELIEF

That there may be separation between the unfit and the pure,
between living creatures that may be eaten and the living creatures
that you are not to eat—

And sometimes I'm out with friends and see them reach
       for a mouthful of whatever
       it is I won't allow myself, a pork chop
       or Caesar with chicken
       or a luscious chocolate torte
       with its risk of insomnia or even (God forbid)
       some "buttery-flavored" spread
And I play the game *what would you do if you were starving*
       and there was nothing left to eat
       except what's on that plate,
       but I know that's just crazy
       talk because (of course) I'd violate every
       rule in the book to save my sorry ass,
Which makes the game a poor measure of my devotion
       to any quasi-tribal, quasi-
       definitive definition of allowability,
       and also to the notion
       that in a time of abundance,
       a little bit of self-restraint goes a long way.
Here's the thing—
       Belief *is a psychological state in which one*
       holds a proposition to be true,
       even in the absence of objective
       (read: scientific, actual) fact, and they –
       psychological states –
       are notoriously, well, psychological,
       able to spin the mind
       towards expectation & artifice
Which is likely how the giant tree Yggradsil found itself
       at the center of Norse cosmology

when it was obvious that our disk-planet
floated like water on oil
under a crust of blue firmament.
(But, wait—
          Didn't Alexander the Great
          see the Earth's curvature
          when carried aloft by giant birds,
          which turned out to be true, despite
          the subpar methodology?)
Anyway. Belief is fixation, but surely it's not impossible
          that there *are* detestable things,
          things created by the Creator
          with unfit flesh, anomalous desires,
          and an unnaturalness about them,
          including cormorants,
          weasels,
          and the aforementioned pig;
Also that fabulous *Kung Pao* shrimp from Lucky Express—
          Also that other guy (you know
          who I'm talking about). That's the theory,
          anyway, that we'll be better humans
          in general and Jews in particular
          if we just lay off whole classes of the lesser
          stuff...
Bottom-feeders & trichinosis & you don't want to put
          your mouth where that thing's been,
          though those are Johnny-
          come-lately explanations for our quest
          after
          just-plain holiness, which itself
          isn't so much about sacred as it is
          about separation,
          a striving that remains at heart
          a kingdom of the psyche,
Vulnerable to sugar pills, hypnosis, and the evil eye.
          As in: too much black bile
          leads to melancholy.

As in: some dead are worthier
of my attention than others,
i.e., *this* chewing, pawing thing
is a knife
in God's throat.
Organic, gluten-free, vegan, raw: there's always
something we can't have,
isn't there,
something we hold at arm's length
because our body is an altar
or because someone (Moses, Mom,
our massage therapist)
intoned the simple mantra,
there are detestable things.
And thus we believe there are detestable things,
even as we steal them
off the plate,
even as we kneel down
beside them and eat.

Sue Swartz

(holiness for moderns)

Holy are you to be, for holy am I, YHWH your God!

Holy is the one who keeps the Sabbath day
and holy the one who picks his own pocket to buy bread.

Holy is the one who turns away from molten idols, and holy
the one who plays poker with unsanctioned deities.

Holy is the one who offers a sacrifice of well-being
and holy the one who sacrifices her being for an open palm.

Holy are those who leave the edges of their fields for the poor
and holy those who garden each narrow plot of heartache.

Holy is the one who does not swear falsely,
and holy the one who swears by intention's cracked mirror.

Holy is one who removes stumbling blocks from before
the blind, and holy the one who forces the deaf to hear.

Holy are those who refuse to traffic in slander
and holy are those who sit in a boxful of scorpions.

Holy are those who do not harvest young fruit, and holy those
who plant caution and impulse with the same plow.

Holy is one who will not eat a thing soaked in blood
and holy the one that finds a menstruating woman beautiful.

Holy are those who do not incise their skin to honor the dead
and holy are those who etch the truth onto each blank page.

Holy is one who refuses to whore his children for cash
and holy the one who does not ornament his child with illusion.

Holy is one who uses weighing stones of equal measure
and holy the one that fills her pitcher with morning's judgment.

Holy is the one who remembers life as a stranger, and holy
the one that gives up her name for a shiver of freedom.

Holy are those who do not mix wool with linen, them with us—
      And holy are those who hold out for perfection
beyond the narrow gates.

(postscript: in the altogether)

To any kin of one's own flesh you are not to come-near,
exposing their nakedness—

A drunken brawl is no excuse, neither
is the tattooed rose between her breasts.

This is the book of a kick to the groin.

Slip your hand inside its pages—

In it, proper party manners.
In it, red stilettos and crisp black chador.

All the ways we signal what belongs to whom.

Mother of, father of, son of, daughter of,
each crevice and curve, curl & freckle.

Of course this is about the nakedness,
the unadorned epidermis, unsheathed skin—

Equally so about the way Adam knew Eve
in paradise, and Isaac knew Rebecca
in his dead mother's tent—

The pleasure & indifference, the meaning
of every small *oh.*

Do not reach for the skirts of your holy sister,
though she is beautiful.

Behind the face that speaks to you—
Do not, in desire, peer.

ATONEMENT

Aaron shall place his hands upon the head of the goat
and confess the iniquities and transgressions of the Israelites—

Each of us has two pockets, our sages say.

One holds a slip of paper—
     All I am is dust and ashes & to dust I shall return.

And one holds a slip of paper—
     The whole world was created just for me.

All wanting ends in dust, cautions the first pocket;
while the second consoles us with the prospect of everything.

But what of the third pocket, slim & hidden, fastened
by a velvet clasp?

Each Yom Kippur, between *we have offended*
and *we have rebelled*, we undo this clasp and lift out
a threadbare message penned by our own hand—

     Sleeper awake! Your list of broken promises
is long, what you leave undone longer still.

Yes, we have built up and torn down.
Yes, we have promised everything and given dust.

So each year between *who by fire* and *who by water*,
we savor this opening where the past falls away
and we are as in our beginning, naked
                  and rife with possibility.

Sue Swartz

All our obligations: not-obligations. All our vows:
not-vows. Set free once more in the endless oasis,
we place the note back in its linen tent—

And goat by lonely goat, we redo the silent clasp.
We Regret. We Atone. We Create anew.

TIME

On six days work may be done, but on the seventh day—

What I hoped to say is on another piece of paper,
scribbled some days back, but then they ran out of coffee
and the parking meter clicked red—

and no spare change in my pockets—

and a pen turned to mud—

And it was a Wednesday, then a Thursday. Ordinary
lists. Things fell through.

Apart. *Religion flies you into buildings—*

Yes, but only if you're so inclined.

Otherwise, we tilt toward the pedestrian,
fill all those *ruthless rapacious* hours with street corner
small talk. The busted traffic light.

Rush to buy envelopes on sale, and then it's another
unaccounted for revolution of Earth.

Flies you into buildings, yes, also—

Full stop straight into the throttle of time.

The clock flipped on its head, head over heels,
whatever metaphor will do, and then—

Stop, full stop. No pencil poised, no key turning.

Frenzy and hangover, payment and debt.

Sue Swartz

How we love each morning's labors. Each evening's rush.
But on the seventh, slowed hand. Quiet sleep.

A day to search for all we have misplaced.

(local time)

That fiftieth year shall be a jubilee for you—

six years prune vineyard sow field slave to ripening rhythm
        one year respite release tempo mastered

seven times seven, matrix of perfect partition

go	go	go	go	go	go	stop
go	go	go	go	go	go	stop
go	go	go	go	go	go	stop
go	go	go	go	go	go	stop
go	go	go	go	go	go	stop
go	go	go	go	go	go	stop
go	go	go	go	go	go	stop
go	go	go	go	go	go	stop

then time outside local time: // STOP full STOP

set your life by this clock of untethering

❧

Undoing, unbecoming—
        Giving it all back.

Consider the simple green bud of self
and within, all our restless fertility.

Consider our short-lived tenancy as its tiller
and tender. How things fall through.

How rest is not loss, still is not fallow.

How to stop without sacrifice.

Sue Swartz

(postcard from the avenue of forgetting)

If you do not hearken to me....
I will destroy your high places, cut down your cult-stands...
Then the land will enjoy its Sabbaths—

Where the Jezreel meets the Jordan is a silent
minaret, entrance gate where we get our tickets stamped.
We act like we're the only ones, but scratch the surface
and discover a familiar tongue. Trowel & dustpan, palm
of speckled dirt—
    And the exuberance of Empire rises up, bullet
& bomb let loose like wild beasts and another palm below,
graceful horses fly across steppe, red banner singing,
crescent unfurled, four centuries of olives figs apricots
grapes—
    And below, Richard's lion heart and jeweled helmet,
crusader of Zion. Below, pottery and poetry, beveled dome
& flowered wadi—
    Below, Gladiator's spiny arm. Trilling acrobat
in tribute to Zeus. Below, gymnasium. Below, colonnade.
Dionysian desire. How long will the familiar last?
    Ask Antiochus of Assyria, Yanni the Hasmonean,
the gangly youth we once were. Below our feet, David's
slingshot. King Saul's head nailed to a Philistine fence.
Below—
    Short sword and throwing spear, mattock, sickle,
chariot and ax. Daughters in virgin robes weep for Mekal,
grand conqueror of Canaan, our land—
    Beisan, Bisan, Nysa, Scythopolis: call this patch
whatever you wish. The past is not a foreign country.
These are not barbarians beneath our feet. In our hands,
the same filthy abattoir—
    The same entrance gate.
One by one we too will vanish from this place, released
into the weedy growth at border's edge—

we who desire

We and all our small talk. We and all our failures.
An entire story of separation. An entire tale of time.

Beit She'an Archaeological Park, Israel

Sue Swartz

DISMANTLING

Sue Swartz

JEWISH TRAVEL

Take a head-count of the entire community of Israel,
by their clans, by their fathers' houses—

The Greeks called the fourth book *Arithmoi*, Numbers,
for they were a Euclidean people, taken with the point-by-point
census of men assembled for battle, tribal banners and silver
trumpets—all bright colors & glorious song.

I'd do the same if the sparkling Aegean was outside my window,
but alas, the Hebrew is clear… We are *ba'midbar*, in the gently hued
and anonymous desert. Mid-morning, early Spring, our small clan
is making its way across fanning fractals of sand.

Twenty minutes out and R. is nervous—
Do we have enough water? How will we get back
to the parking lot without a map?

I think of my father then, how he hated to sit even one block
in traffic. How he would drive the extra mile, make ill-advised
after ill-advised turn just to keep moving. J. says uncertainty is
good for us, that every Jew has a half-packed carryall under the bed.

Hell, our ancestors misplaced an entire generation in this
very desert, jokes B. We meander across a slight gully— I'm sure
we've been here before, but R. says no—

And I think once again of my father, how a lifetime ago
lost in a lattice of backcountry roads, he opened the car window
and yelled Help! into the directionless trees. If I was here then,
I might have already passed the intersection of revelation and thorns.

Surely I would have witnessed all the wilderness has to offer.

Tzin Desert, Israel

(movement)

Set the carrying poles in place—
Remove all the ashes from the altar—
Then the camp can begin its journey—

There is a certain beauty in dismantling.

The wall devoid of photographs…
Dinner plates wrapped in newsprint…

Everything in wary relation to box or bag
or bulging trunk. My mother was a genius of the interstice,
mistress of lopsided geometry, every dip in the road
put right with plastic tarp & packing tape.

Some tenderhearted poet wrote once—
Three moves in 6 months and I remain the same—

But surely he was kidding. The I who today
unfolds the tent corners barely recognizes the I
who took out last Tuesday's trash.

There is certain beauty in dismantling, uncertain
splendor in building up—

Don't get too comfortable, she would advise,
then hand me a suitcase. Inside (where we live),
often nothing but words (what we carry).

You know the more things change, the more
they stay—
Any patch of ground good
as the next for footfall.

(wandering)

On the twentieth day of the second month, the cloud lifted
from the Tabernacle and the Israelites set out on their journey—

Silver trumpets proclaim the shift—

The hour to move forward, the hour to encamp,
On our furtive trek from Sinai to Canaan,
To the land we were promised (freedom).
      The hour to move forward, the hour to encamp,
Back and forth we go, willy-nilly wandering
To the land we were promised (freedom),
Pangs numerous as the stars in heaven.
      Back and forth we go, willy-nilly wandering,
Pulling up stakes, then settling in—
Pangs numerous as the stars in heaven,
We stand at the juncture of burden & craving.
      Pulling up stakes, then settling in—
Our sense of direction has become unhinged.
We stand at the juncture of burden & craving:
(Moaning) *Are we there yet? Are we there yet?*
      Our sense of direction has become unhinged.
At future's ledge, misfortune taunts us—
(Moaning) *Are we there yet? Are we there yet?*
Why oh why did we leave Mother Egypt?
      At future's ledge, misfortune taunts us—
Throats dry from proclaiming yes.
Why oh why did we leave Mother Egypt,
With its onions, garlic, and pots of meat?
      Throats dry from proclaiming *yes.*
This is the end to all pleasant constriction,
All the onions, garlic, and pots of meat.
Bound are we to this labyrinth of sand.
      This is the end to all pleasant constriction
Commands the God of moving tents.

Bound are you to this labyrinth of sand,
The everlasting wilderness, its sinuous song.
        So commands the God of moving tents:
Get used to your burden, your craving, your fear,
The everlasting wilderness, its sinuous song.
On your furtive trek from slavery to freedom
        As silver trumpets proclaim the shift—

NO OTHERS BEFORE ME

The Levites shall be mine.

For every god—
      Favorites.

Zeus had Io. Diana,
the chaste and ring-shaped moon.
Ishtar had a hankering
for herd-boy and stallion,
and let's not forget: Noah
& Jonah & Mary & Job.

Chosen. Chosen among chosen.
Divine head over heels.

Io was turned into a cow
for her troubles, the stallion pursued
by thong and whip.

As for the rest—

A litany of guilty pleasure.
For the keepers and carriers
of holy swag, so many sad stories
to tell around the water cooler.

True or false—

Suitor or servant,
      but not both.
Lover or supplicant,
      but not both.
Keeper or kept,
      but not both.

Might as well admit it,
you're addicted to love.

Sue Swartz

(abstention)

If anyone, man or woman, explicitly utters a Nazirite's vow,
to set himself apart for God—

This is the book of little white lies—

In it, the cut-off truth and Dionysian vine.
In it, all the ways we vow to make it right.

Status is earned by what is left undone:

Grape soda gone flat on the counter,
scissors rusted shut in the sink.

And this is the book of self & sinner—

In it, the bit of Delilah in every gal.
In it, floral libation. Muscular desire.

How we mark & hallow our wretchedness—

When something unimagined.
When something unsayable.

Awash in the nature of the plain & obvious
(might as well admit it)—

How badly we want to be loved.
How badly we love to tear it down.

(the loudest self)

Miriam and Aaron spoke against Moses because of the Cushite
woman he had married… She was stricken with tzara'at—

Miriam:

    Some remember the reed and pitch basket set afloat
in the Nile, my cleverness in addressing Pharaoh's daughter with a voice
melodic as rippling tides, self-effacing enough to avert my brother's fate.

    (I dreamt that love without tyranny is possible.)

and some remember the rhapsodic celebration before the parted sea,
a women's chorus of yearning, skin salty from the passage, body
exhausted from dance, tongue atremble with freedom.

Some remember my flowing wells in the desert, sustenance burst from
my aching heart, how the people cast their buckets low, how billowy phlox
sprung from the arid land where I walked—

    (The worst immorality is to believe in nothing.)

and others remember what has been lost (the love of brothers, wide and
comfortable bed). How God's taunts penetrate to the bone. *Loud girl,*
brazen girl: how bitter still waters become.

Now I cling to the truth sprouting wild in my head, the rush of words.
In the borderland that has become my true address, I linger—

    (I have been asked why I am myself—)

In solitude. Birthing what the wilderness demands, and I tell you
there is nothing sweeter in all the narrow world.

❦

Aaron:

We hurled our disquietude into the fire and out came
dreadful reproach. Could you blame ~~us~~ her?

The hunger, the troubles, the never-ending sand—
The demands for water, the pathways of perfumed phlox—
His wrought-up wife, every bitter pill assigned—

Clearly, she'd come undone.

Brother, I cannot stand the sound of our sister falling.

I beseech you:
  Untangle this tangled web of misplaced ~~rebuke~~ love.

❦

Moses:

In the end, of course, none of it is fair:
the yearning, the regret, the choice.

And worse yet (*O God, heal her!*)—

Will no one ever understand me?

❦

Beautiful! Beautiful! upon her return.

DOUBT WITHOUT END

Moses sent them to scout the land of Canaan and said to them,
Go up through the Negev and then up to the hill country. See
the land, what it is and the people settled in it—

1.

In a perfect world, I would be able to convince you
of this—
        You cannot stay where you are.

Look! The season's first grapes, the lush
pomegranates and figs. The eye tears up with pleasure.

This fruit is safe to eat. Do not abstain.

Something, somewhere, is approaching with
your future.

2.

Enemies—

Anakites. Amalekites.
Hittites. Jebusites.
Amorites. Canaanites—

Giants all.
Also, our terrible
       imagining.

We cannot.
Will not.
Must not
      cross over.

Sue Swartz

How grand our fears.
How small our defenses.

(*A doubt without end
is not even a doubt.*)

3.

Your corpses, yours, will fall in this wilderness.

You were young once.
Recall the garden. The rainbow.
Going forth and circling back.
Recall the flocks of ministering angels;
          the pit, its deep focus and rim—
Your endless appetite,
circling and circling.

The book of what you dreamt.
The book of darkness, bucket of live coals.
Recall roaring armies,
and salty, salty passage.

You were young once.
Now you meander
with a small & ragged map
through a valley of sand.
Endless story of endless sand!
Something, somewhere
is approaching.

There is a key dangling
from your ragged map, cold
to the touch. Your children will use it
          to enter.

4.

If we could have back our dead, would we ply them
with milk and honey & ask: *What is it like on the other side?*
Would we reminisce over their untimely end?
Laugh together over earthly worries stacked up like dirty dishes?
Be tough enough to pocket one small bit of advice?
Yes, yes, yes, and likely not.

Face it. Our cowardice exceeds our curiosity.
This, then, is our punishment—
To know nothing would be different, even if we knew
            everything.
We would not use our ignorance more wisely.
Time would still pass through us unattended.
Silence is what we want from the dead. Have pity on us,
we say. Do not remind us just what kind of country this is.

PRAISE THE CONTRARY &
ITS DEFENDERS

Now Korach rose up before Moses together with 250 Israelites—

For the chief musician, on common instrument:
A song of rebellion.

Praise rising up. Praise unlawful assembly. Praise the road of excess
and the palace of wisdom. Praise glass houses & the hand
that cradles the stone.

Praise Galileo. Praise acceleration.
Praise the medium and the message.
Praise en masse and the pull of a straight line.
Praise outside agitators
and inside jobs. Praise Red Emma. Praise Joan of Arc.

Praise wayward daughters and praise, praise their wayward sons.

Praise the power of indulgence. Praise Luther's *Ninety-Five Theses*.
Praise the nail and the printing press. Praise free verse.
Praise the First Amendment.
Praise illicit beauty, yellow sunflowers and red wheelbarrows.
Praise the poets of Guantanamo.

Praise the noisy midnight streets.
Praise the crazy birds at dawn and praise their woven nests.
Praise Isaac Newton. Praise the apple.

Praise *Letters from Prison*. Praise the bound notebook and what
is found within. Praise Legal Aid attorneys. Praise kitchen-table
conspiracies. Praise our hunger and the days we are the bread.

Praise farmers' markets. Praise heirloom tomatoes,
Al Gore and quantum physics. Praise Schrödinger and praise his cat.
Praise talking snakes. Praise run-on sentences.

Praise the best minds of any generation. Praise other people's poems, especially the fickle and freckled. Praise Norma Jean. Praise standing on the table. Praise John Brown and all that trouble in river city.

Praise Walt Whitman & Jimi Hendrix. Praise the body's wild intelligence. *Praise the giraffe and the porcupine.* Praise getting satisfaction. Praise cross-dressing. Praise untouchables, undesirables, partisans and riffraff. Praise slackers.

Praise those who talk back. Praise sympathy for the devil. Praise mothers of *the disappeared.* Praise mothers of the found. Praise Planned Parenthood and the siren song.

Praise singers and psalm-makers, Freud and Sinatra. Praise Gertrude Stein and all thirteen ways of looking at that blackbird.

Praise nude beaches. Praise the terrible twos. Praise hitting your head against the wall. Praise giving peace a chance. Praise Selma, Alabama. Praise the Abraham Lincoln Brigades. Praise Sacco and Vanzetti. Praise Jobs & Curie. Praise Einstein and his bad posture.

Praise *Buffy the Vampire Slayer.* Praise crossing party lines. Praise playing footsy under the table. Praise street puppets and LSD and stealing this poem. Praise backyard whiskey.

Praise Priscilla the Monkey Girl. Praise her admirers. Praise Earhart and those who remember what they are told to forget. Praise agnostics.

Praise what we are not supposed to praise. Praise the electrical storm and the still small voice. Praise all the proverbs of hell. *Praise this feeling of trying to write about the truth.*

Praise those who see it coming. Praise those who do it anyway. Praise what swallows us whole.

Praise what happens next.

　　　　Sue Swartz

(related interludes)

For wrath has gone forth from God: the plague has begun!

Any resemblance to people or deaths depicted here is fiction, pure
fiction—
For how else could we continue to believe—
To imagine we know what stands between life and death—
That there is a line, no matter how slim, between murder and miracle—
That the bones of our rebellion will be pure, right, good?

❦

They came upon a man gathering wood on the Sabbath day—

He was sentenced to die for this violation.
No matter he had a sick wife.
No matter it was difficult to break the habit of slavish work.
Someone picked up that first stone, someone the second—
The earth is full of such hands, of such fallen bodies.
The stones themselves are not to blame.

Dear man—
        Dear bloodied man: this is the way of sacred freedom.

❦

Instruct them to make fringes on the corners of their garments—

So much to remember, all 613 ways the body can mutiny,
the mind slip into reverie—

Dear sinner—
        Dear reader: Gather the fringe up in your hand.

Like an ambulance outside a sick house is the thin umbilical
of blue. Caress each knot as the call goes out.

THE WATER FINDS ITS WAY

(G)ather up the ashes of the (red) heifer and deposit them…
in a clean place as a water of lustration—

The spring melt has begun. The water finds its way down
    New Street, down the pasty, potholed alleyways of Grodno,
    past the terse eyes of her citizens, uncovering untoward gifts
    buried deep in winter's bitterness.
Chipped headstone, polished bone, gold-capped tooth.
    With each sunrise comes another melting. This is the ritual.
He who shot Goldschmid for smuggling a jar of milk is unclean.
    He who ordered Skibelski to dance in clown's hat while
    marching him to die is unclean. So too he who wrapped
    yellow cloth around the arm of Freydowicz, smirking.
Unclean. He who murdered Abramovitz on a Sunday, Badilkes
    near the brick works, and Prenska six months along
    is unclean. He who legislated that Jewish boots could not
    trespass sidewalks meant for Christian feet, unclean.
So too he who hung Spindler, hung Drucker, hung Kimcher.
    A knuckle. A sphenoid. With each sunrise comes
    another un-covering. The water finds its way.
He who shuttered the city tight against survivors is unclean.
    He who plowed under patterned headstones
    to erect a stadium, a place for applause and song
    on the bones of the dead is unclean.
With each melting comes another flood. Another story.
    He who patched up potholes with rich soil dug
    from under the cheering stadium is unclean.
Those who admonished the orange-clad work crews
    to quickly, *quickly*, sweep away the errant
    jawbones, unclean. And those who walk down
    replenished streets smoking a cigarette as if
    no one was murdered there is unclean.
With each melting comes another reminder.
    Do not count on the sun's drying rays.

Do not imagine these dead will acquiesce.
You will re-bury them. They will surge. Pave over
    them. They will rush through the tiniest
    cracks, turn fields to swamp, topple
    the tree of forgetfulness
    planted by your own
    muddy hand.

Grodno, Belarus, July 2003

(death flows)

Miriam died there and was buried there—
Aaron breathed his last—

We are deep now
      ba'midbar, in the gently hued
and implacable desert.

The last of who we were
      will be buried in its sand
(wandering remnant,
bedrock of what cannot be known).

First sister, then brother,
      no one is immune. All must
cross through, cross over.

A torrent
      of losing. Separation
from the truest twin.

Revision of the way
      things were supposed to go
(pummel the rock or heave it
in anger—
      it's all the same).

The verdict
      washes us clean. Strips us
down to the bone. Death flows
like a river through this story.

LANDLORD TO SUCH A MULTITUDE

How fair are your tents, O Jacob, your dwelling places, O Israel!

(Inside me, a house.)

In my house, King David plucks his lonesome harp
as Queen Esther prances in royal robes. The newly freed burst
into splendid song. A young man in black wool coat *shuckles*,
while his twin casually cradles a whirling dervish of a gun,
and Emma Goldman gathers up crumbs of manna in my house.
Chomsky dukes it out with Dershowitz, Spinoza compares notes
with Steinem. Narrow-eyed survivors perch with silent accusation
and Jews turned other taunt with their choosing. In my house,
women pass Friday's hands over flame, cover ankles modestly.
So too, in my house, women chant Torah no matter the day
of the month. Here live socialists and secularists, *ba'alei teshuvah*,
and un-decideds. Ethiopians crowd into rooms already jumbled
tight with Russians, Moroccans, and former Episcopalians.
Chickpeas and olives are hoarded, some pieces of matzo, a bowl
of borscht. Bacon. The dying are everywhere – from pogrom
and heavenly plague, loneliness and home–made bomb.
In my house, elders exhort the young to never forget. Rukeyser
gifts us the 20th Century, the radio blasts *Hatikvah* & Winehouse,
Ramone & Streisand. Madoff speculates, Einstein calculates,
and Baruch Goldstein plots his gallows revenge. Old women
play Mah Jongg, and everyone quotes scripture out of context.
There are hamsas, yoga mats and two sets of dishes. Furniture
is rearranged daily in my house. Walls change their hue.
Strangers dance together at midnight with outstretched arms,
tussle at dawn with mighty fists.
(Inside me, a house. Inside the house,
bickering boarders. Inside the house, rent always coming due).

WE WHO DESIRE

(Pinchas) stabbed the Israelite man and the Moabite woman in the belly....because he was zealous for his God—

Before   white phosphorous illumined the bodies of the cursed,
tunnels imploded with quarrel and armament—

Before   mortar shells & Qassam rockets, F-16 bombers & Apache
helicopters, cast lead and the clotted remnants of sacrifice—

Before   *all this is rightfully ours* and the taste of the morgue,
artillery fire and hollowed-out orchards—

Before   mirrors of pain and while preparing food for the baby,
strategic landscape and alleyways of blue ash—

Before   children found alive beside their mother's scalded body

                and the keening that swallows up the future—

Before   shrapnel in the stomach and are you sure he's dead,

Before   terrible, terrible thirst for the forbidden sea—

Before   *Blessed is the will of the Lord* which today guides the hand
of the bombardier, guides the hand of the apologist
and the commander,

Before   the hand, unclaimed, that fed sheep at dawn—

Before   human shields, crackling static, and the strangled sirens
in their graceful flight—

Deep   in our wandering, sick with desire, we cried out *Choose us!*

Sue Swartz

Creator of light and shatterer of worlds – let us prove
ourselves to you.

Thus   deep in the night did we ascend with our offering.

              deep in the night did we pick up the sword.

(and this desire as well)

Rightly speak the daughters of Zeloph'had!

Deep in the wandering come the daughters of Zeloph'had.
They stand before Moses   & the High Priest
before the gray-haired Elders   & the entire community

and do not flinch. They bring
no theory   no dogma   no theology

Only the hum of uncertainty—
     Why should our father's land be lost to us
     and all who come after just because
     there is no son?

They rise before all Israel   before all history
to say give us a holding. On razor thin circumstance
these daughters balance, they and all their descendants—

union maids   women's libbers   grrrl gangs
& the one who says *you can make your own damned dinner,*
I'm going out with the girls.

All of them and all of us   all of theirs & all of ours
perch before the Holy Tent   before the Elders.

We stand and do not flinch   but wait.
Wait for a God we can believe in.

Sue Swartz

POSSESSING

Sue Swartz

AND THESE ARE THE WORDS

On the first day of the eleventh month in the fortieth year, Moses spoke to the Israelites regarding all that God had commanded—

1.

This is the book of sayings and things,
what is made real by our telling.

In it: our story is *the* story.
In it: allusion we cannot grasp.

And this is the book of incidents & accidents,
where God came in person to say—

Where floating out there, tumbling
down there—

Where repetition raises an arc of desire
and we spiral back—

2.

We were nothing at first.
Then the story found us.

We were young once—

Dust before we were multitudes.
Blueprint before we were steel.

Every \stôr-ē\ is like this story:
part rousing prophecy, part iron furnace.

3.

I am an experiment.
I am a recipient.
Preservationist. Translator. Monument.
I remember it though I was not there.
Saw it with my own eyes.
I am a mnemonic.
I am a mosaic. Off-key chorale.

I am a time machine.
A telegraph tapping
            from my mouth to your ear—
History, taxonomy, fragment, reprise.
Does it matter if the words are true
or truth or truer still?

I am a schematic.
I am a joist.
Bastard vernacular. Everything begot.
I am revelation and bad relation,
an encyclopedia of this and that.
Both/and. Either/or.
Enclosure, torment, skeleton, key.

I am a reader.
I am the text.

On my knees in the paper temple.

4.

This is the book of annotation.

In it, we rewrite the way back.
In it, we wander out loud—

Each of us a syllable trying
to understand.

(plot summary)

Face to face the Lord spoke to you on the mountain
out of the fire—

we were unbound then
when lightening
scorched our heels
when freedom
bleached us blind
when endless wanting
exploded
the wilderness
ours and not-ours
the hunger
ours and not-ours
the table set
sound we could not
grasp
hamper of fire
we could not put down
how to speak of this—

the sweep of inattention
all we did not
understand
all we did not hear
as we stumbled
into the un-
crossable
unknowable
how to speak of—

at home or on the way
lying down rising up

we were there
when trumpets roared
will perish
outside
the bordered land
there is no other finale
this is the instruction
what we made
of endless wanting
to our children
we will tell it
tell it

Sue Swartz

(possession)

You shall take possession of the land and settle in it—

This is the book of anticipation.
In it, we have reached the place
just outside the place
                                    where—

And this is the book of our
children's children. We no longer
recognize ourselves on its pages.

This is the tome of sacred freedom—

& the chapter of coming to pass.
In it, the compulsion to keep on
keeping on.

In it, we change. Rules change.
Someone puts a map in our hand.

Someone a sword.

❦

This is the part we hate to admit—

How easy it is to pick up the rock,
put up with other people's suffering.

~~Anakites. Amalekites.~~
~~Hittites. Jebusites.~~
~~Amorites. Canaanites.~~

Giants all, undone by our imagining,
the terrible pleasure of devoting them
to destruction—

Imagine it—

(charred bodies intertwined like the roots of a tree—
(man and woman young and old ox sheep ass with the edge of the
sword—
(shoot people with neither money nor cellphones to give—
(tear down their altars cut down their sacred posts—
(strike the boy with the butt of a rifle until he falls to the dirt path—
(assailants wielding knives storm the railway station—
(put them to death and hang them on five trees—
(bombings kill 13 and wound 10 in an attack on a polio vaccination
team—

Cause their name to perish from under heaven—)

How we hate to talk about it:
the wild beast etched deep inside.

❧

we were unbound then
when the earth cracked open
and blood rushed out
unbound then
when signs & portents
when province & providence
engulfed   outdid
the barbarous
the ominous
undeniable others
in our way

how to speak of—

the sound
we could not grasp
the unknowable
we came to know

how we *reached the place*
where death stands waiting

how we reached it
and survived

STORE UP THESE WORDS OF MINE

Safeguard and keep this entire Instruction—
In the land that YHWH, God of your ancestors, is giving you—

Be a *genizah*, an alcove beyond the eaves, repository,
arsenal where the great deep has made its will known.

Be a storage locker, tape recorder, silver ampule
for every breathless phoneme, penny from heaven.

Be locked and loaded, true and blue, keeper kept.
Be an attaché where milk & honey, where earth pushes
        up against paradise—

❦

do not plant an *ashera* tree // luxuriant consort of green
do not raise a standing stone in phallic opposition
do not offer up blemish or defect // this is the law of perfection
do not prostrate to other gods to sun moon sky: stone them
do not rely on only one witness // by the word of many: stone them
stone those who lure you   brother sister mother son
stone them pierce them   wife servant neighbor self
do not imagine yourself Levite though you be a nation of priests
do not cross back to Egypt // to you that way is closed
do not choose a foreign tsar // bow to brother father kin
do not multiply imperial wives nor gold horses silver
do not cross your offspring through fire do not seek after ghosts
do not inquire after the dead do not augur or enchant
do not abide by false prophets: noisy children with pointed twigs
do not let your heart go soft // do what needs to be done
        do not send to war those with a new house
        do not send to war those with a new vineyard
        do not send to war those with a new bride

do not send to war those who will not kill
do not fight without offering peace // forced-labor in place of death
do not strike down women babes // only men with the edge of the sword
do not forget your birthright ~~Hittite Amorite Canaanite~~
do not leave breath in them ~~Perizzite Anakite Jebusite~~
do not murder trees like men or capture a woman willy-nilly
do not suffer a rebel and drunkard // even your child: stone him
do not let-hang the condemned overnight // even a criminal: bury him
do not keep a wayward donkey do not risk a shattered roof
do not dress in women's clothing   do not yoke wool to flax
do not serve hoopoe snail eel bat // knife in God's throat
do not cook a kid in suckling milk nor take a mother with her young
do not charge non-virginity // her garment will be spread in proof
do not pretend sexual purity // even your daughter: stone her
do not sleep with the wife of your friend // ever // no never
do not remain silent during rape // cry out though silence responds
do not disgrace a virgin without prospect: she is yours
do not snub your brothers' wife // also yours
do not marry a wife you once spurned // do not seize a man below
do not allow a bastard to enter // barred for ten generations
do not allow Ammonite or Moabite: for the ages bid them ill
do not expose your animal self do not prostitute your flesh
do not mix your weighing stones do not prolong your neighbor's sorrow
      do not tether the needy   or close your hand
      do not charge interest to kin   or sickle another's grain
      do not ask unfair collateral   or testify in malice
      do not seize a widow's cloak   or move your neighbor's boundary
      do not add whip-strokes   or muzzle a threshing ox
its hunger important as yours // for you were slaves in Egypt
do not drive out Amalek from this story: obliterate his name
do not forget to remember   eye for eye / life for life

❦

hands moving under the sun   bodies of the nameless
slaughter your springtime sacrifice   break the bread of affliction
rejoice in the place God chooses   you are the beloved

gather three times to dedicate   chosen among chosen
do not come empty-handed   first-fruits of redemption
       praise the strong hand // outstretched arm
       praise crossing over // milk and honey
             rejoice rejoice
do not eat in sorrow   this soil is yours
do not eat in sorrow   you are my testimony

Sue Swartz

JUSTICE // JUSTICE

Justice, justice you shall pursue.

This is an animal poem,
feral & hungry & desperate for meat.

This is a poem that says without blinking:
I want him dead—
                then hesitates.

This is a bare-breasted poem, blind
and unmoved by bitter desire.

This is a poem with too many *thes*—
The man holding the rifle.
The man dead in the field.
The barricades. The artillery.
The wooden crosses.

It wants to sue for damages.
It may yet do what is right.

This poem almost went nameless,
but wanted the satisfaction that comes
with specificity—
                which man was holding
the gun, which man was not.

This is an orderly poem, begun
somewhere in the middle.

And ending there.

This poem over-identifies with its subject—
            a young man burned alive
            inside a church—

Yet knows there are two sides
to every one.

This is a bleeding-heart poem, believing
as it does in the rule of law.

It is a contrary poem, an eye
for eye poem, an Amnesty International
poem.

This poem holds sin in the palm of its hand.

Also a city of refuge,
all sapphire streets and glistening kindness.

This is an arithmetic poem—
            counting loss and lunacy—

And a cultured poem. It has read Adorno
& Reznikoff, is beholden to neither.

This is a poem without final verdict—
                a shameless thing,
living off the why and the what and the who-
is-to-blame.

This may be a useless poem.

It will do nothing in its short life,
a penny that collects at the bottom of things.

This is a poem that bites the hand.

It thrills to throw the first jagged stone,
consumed by every slight and foe.

This poem is ransom note and calling card,
petty thief and hard-hearted bitch.

Tomorrow it may be
a graying matron in worn dress
tending her tomato plants.

It may turn Judas and forget to act nice.

It strains to whisper *evil*
over and over, over and over into your ear.

This poem will not be easy.
This poem will not be silent.

(if we lived in this house)

You shall pronounce the blessing at Mount Gerizim
and the curse at Mount Eval—

Springtime in the hills above Nablus.
        Mountain calls across
        the green-and-brown slash
        of city below
        to mountain on the other side,
        calls, then recants,
        then calls again (despondent)
        you are always turning away,
        while we, tourists
        in this land of contested inheritance,
        zigzag across the slant & slope
        in our rental car, headed
        toward the easy intoxication
        of unfamiliar ritual.
Every diversion in its set season.
        The crowd gathers
        atop Mount Gerizim to wait—
             what will happen next—
        and thus wanders
        into the hollows of history,
        giddy on this appointed day
        of slaughter
        and unleavened bread.
Human hands feed the fire.
        Dror parks the car suddenly,
        sensing an invisible threshold,
        and we pile out,
        Mount Eval at our backs.
        Off we go to welcome
        the entrance of the 131st
        Samaritan High Priest, to gasp

and gawk as a hundred men
dressed in white robes
slit, on cue,
the throats
of unblemished sheep,
feed the flames
as the expectant hillside erupts—
jubilant.
Springtime in the hills where time stops.
We walk back to the car
in satisfied silence, ignore
Hagit's cell as it rings once,
twice, interrupting
our animal reverie
with buzzing reproach & reminder
of all we would give up
if we truly lived in this house
we did not build,
and soon we are laughing again—
wasn't that a crazy day—
and Dror points the car
downhill
toward the promised land
of what we know.
The sun is red with easy license as we drive.
Through Huwwara
checkpoint, past
a dozen in line on the other side,
the far side, their eyes
set on young Israeli soldiers—
the only ones
who can give them permission
to cross—
and mountain moans
from our ease of forgetting,
our inability to be another people:
You are always turning away.

COVENANT

This day you are becoming a people to YHWH your God—
If you do not hearken to the voice of YHWH your God—

Some days this thought comforts me—
      That we refused to hearken. That we ate our meat
boiled in mother's milk and went whoring after other gods.

That even with a mountain held over our heads, we hesitated.

That's what I tell myself on mornings when I don't know
my right hand from my left. When I open the whole fallen book of
wilted flowers—
      Truck driver shot on his way to get a doughnut.
Boy holding a pickaxe, his life unfolding inside a life meant for men.

      (What kind of god—)

Because I woke again trying to make a small amount of sense
out of the revealed world. Because I'm a one-eyed conscript
in this fraying assembly.

Because I'm panting like an arid field, searching for shade.

I've tried raising my hands over my head. I've held my breath,
plugged my ears & drunk slowly through a straw—
      And still the glitches keep coming.

It's hard not to be defensive. Hard to defend my naiveté.

      (What kind of people—)

Thundering sky, crisp lightning of missile fire.
Anonymous street where a new instruction is written—
Scarlet ash on metal doorknob, human soot and splintered

glass. Windows ripped off hinges, eateries ripped off
                    street corners, owners split while stirring soup.

Forgive us. Pardon us. Surely, we did not mean to—
          A mother incinerated with her young.

Such is the changing circumstance of covenant. The world
will find us, and the why as well. Blood was witness
          to the beginning and favored witness still.

          (Did we walk away—)

I've tried apostasy. I've tried theodicy. *The vale of soul-
making* and every special theory of relativity. The moments
of doubt keep coming.

Good things happen to bad people.

I won't bore you with the list; the proof is in the pudding.
Mountain's turned into a slippery slope and there's no shortage of
fine print—
          Fish in the forest. Emptiness raised up like a tower.
          There's more than enough blame to go around.

          (Did we walk away or did you—)

A house was built, but no one dwells in it. A lover betrothed,
but another rumples the sheets.

Here's the flat-out plague of it—
          Centuries burst forth from our loins and still the deal
remains a deal. We are a people. We heard a voice.

Rain may turn to dust, avenues clot with fading signs,
someone lived here once.
          But what is the meaning of *someone?* The meaning
          of *once?*

And who is the beauty lying next to you, cluster
of henna flowers in her hair?

This, then that, no longer holds. Who believed in it, anyway?

(Together pressed up against the knife—)

Something unsettled is moving toward us: a storm a taking apart a
rhythm not easily contained.

By us, I mean the signatories.

Each groping about in darkness. Each longing to be loved
for who they are.

Sue Swartz

(were it not for)

Be careful to perform all the words of this Torah, for it is not an empty thing for you, it is your life...

I would welcome an easy forgetting, were it not for the words.
I would pass up allotment and ceremony, but never sever the words.

Presence, absence, glory & thunder, ink with great resiliency.
Velvet-wrapped, indelible test, my self bows before the words.

Transcendence is surely a bonus and I'm not after equanimity.
I prefer uproar, wild beasts set loose in the Garden of Words.

Ancient scrolls survive, thrive on impudent twists of commentary.
Turn and turn the story, and the story (in turn) turns our words.

Oh, to be the prime redactor, creator of numinous melancholy.
Lowly poet, heretic, seeker, I lay down and rise up with the words.

The believer in me undecided, blessed with the curse of ambiguity.
Perilous to parse shards like this, endless swooning over the words.

The prophet's heart is a raging fire, helpless before God's word.
I'd burn too, wandering and blue, were it not for the glorious words.

(infinite in all directions)

God let (Moses) see all the land—

This is the book of face to face.
In it, curved throat of god brought close.

In it, nothing remains itself very long.

Our fingerprints are all over its pages,
our minds' lathe spinning and spinning—

Dear reader, dear dizzied reader:
Enjoy the circumnavigation.

I will not lie. There are easier ways
to make a life. But this is your only one—

Do not disappear yourself from it.

❦

& it was evening and it was morning,
a hundred hundred perfections arrayed
in all their fertile expanse—

all the lands we permit ourselves not to see,
pointed twig and the intention of—

so the instructions are in a foreign tongue
so the skies melt in our hands

let us praise the wild and waste,
the floating out there, tumbling down there
beyond

Sue Swartz

you said let there be and there was

we said let there be and there was

❧

Like a pencil poised for calculation—
A key not yet turned in the twitchy ignition—

NOTES

(this and that God created us)
Bone from my bones! Flesh from my flesh… Genesis 2:23
She's come undone…. Song lyrics by Randy Bachman
Creator, shall I bloom? Emily Dickinson, "God Made A Little Gentian"

(catastrophe)
One can live without having survived— Carolyn Forche, "Blue Hour"

(with reference to our conflicting desires)
In memory of conjoined twins Ladan and Laleh Bijani, who died on the operating table, July 2003, after 50 hours of surgery to separate them.

(Isaac's eyes were dimmed)
There is no absence that cannot be replaced, Rene Char, "Chain"

Sleep on a Bed of Stones
For one account of the disastrous climbing season on Everest, see Jon Krakauer's *Into Thin Air*
Everything is foreseen, though free will is given, Pirkei Avot 3:15

(appetite)
On the Cover of the Rolling Stone – lyrics Shel Silverstein, from a song of the same title
Ebudae into Khartoum – lyrics by Enya, "Orinoco Flow"

Nameless
All first person accounts (in italics) from the website Free the Slaves, www.freetheslaves.net.

(what is held within)
On December 13, 2010, fire swept a garment factory north of Dhaka, Bangladesh. Most of the 20 dead and dozens injured were young women. Seven women were killed in January 2013 when they were unable to escape a second floor fire at Smart Fashions, also in Dhaka; two months earlier, 112 died in a blaze at Tazreen Fashions, supplier to many US retailers.

(live your way into the answer):
Title quote (live your way…) – Rainer Maria Rilke, "Letters to a Young Poet #4"
Against this, that – Carolyn Forche, "Blue Hour"
Because the crack in everything – Leonard Cohen, "Anthem"
Chained in some fool's backyard: barking and barking – Tony Hoagland, "Personal"
I cannot live on tomorrow's bread – Langston Hughes, "Democracy"

Love supreme – John Coltrane
Permeable world – Rachel Barenblat, "Permeable World"

PLAGUES
The line dividing good and evil runs through the heart of every human being –
Aleksandr Solzhenitsyn, Gulag Archipelago

APOLOGIA
For my grandchildren – Jacob, Rami, Eliot, and Ruth Anne

(after the glory)
To put it down is forbidden – Alicia Ostriker, "Volcano"

(explanation after the calf):
All there is to know of love we learned from your back – after Karen Alkalay-Gut,
"Dividing"

LET THEM BUILD ME A HOLY PLACE
Referencing the photograph "Lunch Atop a Skyscraper," taken in 1932 during
construction of the former RCA Building. Photographer unknown, though
often assumed to be Charles Ebbets.

(mutable cloud)
Ralph Waldo Emerson, Essays – First Series: *Nature is a mutable cloud which is
never and always the same.*

CLEAN
The Hebrew word *tza'ra'at* is often translated simplistically as leprosy.
The heartbeat on its little wheels! Jorie Graham, "Belief System"
"Power Company Buys Ohio River Village Plagued by Clouds of Acid."
Associated Press, April 17, 2002. The village, with a 2000 population of 221
people, was plagued by sulfurous gas and acid rain from a nearby coal-fired
power plant. American Energy reached a $20 million settlement with residents
to purchase the entire town.
...a spalling of plaster; complete destruction – United States Strategic Bombing
Survey in Hiroshima and Nagasaki, 1945

(postscript: in the altogether)
Behind the face that speaks to you – After Emmanuel Levinas

ATONEMENT
The notion of having two pockets is attributed to Rabbi Bunim of P'shiskha,
based on words from Genesis and Talmud.

TIME
Religion flies you into buildings— Victor Stenger. The full quote is "Science flies you to the moon. Religion flies you into buildings."
...ruthless rapacious – C.K. Williams, "Rats"

(movement)
Three moves in 6 months and I remain the same – John Logan, "Three Moves"

NO OTHERS BEFORE ME
Might as well admit it, you're addicted to love – Lyrics by Robert Palmer, "Addicted to Love"

THE LOUDEST SELF
All quotes from Andrea Dworkin
I dreamt that love without tyranny is possible. "First Love"
The worst immorality is to believe in nothing. Heartbreak
I have been asked why I am myself— Heartbreak. The full quote is "I have been asked, politely and not so politely, why I am myself."

DOUBT WITHOUT END
In a perfect world, I would be able to convince you of this – Anna Moschovakis, "prologue"
A doubt without end is not even a doubt – Ludwig Wittgenstein, "On Certainty"

PRAISE THE CONTRARY AND ITS DEFENDERS
praise giraffe and porcupine and *praise this feeling of trying to write about the truth*– Jennifer Michael Hecht, "No I Would Not Leave You If You Suddenly Found God"

WE WHO DESIRE
Written after the 2009 war between Israel and Hamas, known to the Israelis as Operation Cast Lead.

AND THESE ARE THE WORDS
paper temple – Marie Deer, draft of "Deep in the Book House"

(possession)
All lines in italics taken from the *Book of Joshua*, chapters 7 and 8, or from on-line news sources during the week of March 23, 2014.
reached the place where death stands waiting – from the "Warrior Song", Omaha Nation

JUSTICE // JUSTICE
Written immediately after the arrest of Radovan Karadzic in 2008. Any dictator will do.

(if we lived in this house)
The Samaritans, numbering just over 700 people, live atop Mount Gerizim in
Israel and claim to worship in the manner of the ancient Israelites prior to the
Babylonian exile.

COVENANT
the vale of soul-making – John Keats, letter to George and Georgiana Keats, 1819
someone lived here once – written on the walls of houses in Haifa, Israel, by
former Palestinian occupants, often accompanied by photographs of families

ACKNOWLEDGMENTS

Thanks to the following publications, in which some of this book's poems appeared, many in earlier versions or with different titles.

5 a.m.: "Jewish Travel"
Celebrating Seventy: editor Jenny Kander (Wind Press), "...diagnosis / Clean..."
Cutthroat: A Journal of the Arts: "with reference to our conflicting desires"
Drash, Northwest Mosaic: "Anatomy of The Thigh", "...explanation after the calf...", "What the Day Cannot Contain"
Gumball Poetry: "Sleep on a Bed of Stones"
Isotope Magazine: "Entropy/Faith"
Jewish Currents: "The Water Finds Its Way"
Jewish Writing Project: "...were it not for..."
Jews.: "this and that God created us"
Lilith Magazine: "Landlord to Such a Multitude"
Poetica: "Atonement," "Elegy"
Referential: "And Those Are The Words," "Live Your Way Into the Answer," "(mutable cloud)"
Scribblers on the Roof: "Apologia"
Smartish Pace: "On the Eighth Day"
Trivia, Voices of Feminism: "...the loudest self..."
Wayfarer: "Creation", "Movement"

"what is held within" was a finalist for the Rita Dove Poetry Award.

"Praise the Contrary and its Defenders" first appeared in *The Velveteen Rabbi's Passover Haggadah*, version 8

Much gratitude goes to Hedgebrook: Women Authoring Change retreat center for awarding me a residency where the idea for this book was nurtured and many of these poems begun.

More poetry from

Ben Yehuda Press

Open My Lips

Prayers and Poems

Rachel Barenblat

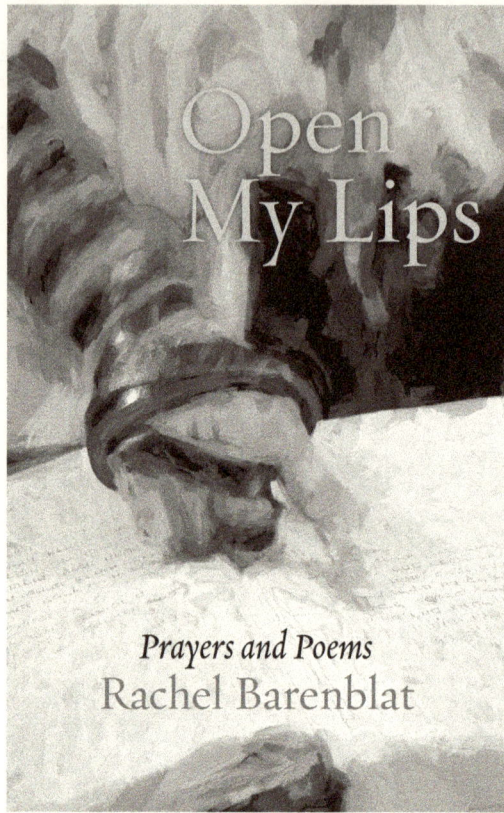

"Barenblat's God is a personal God - one who lets her cry on His shoulder, and who rocks her like a colicky baby. These poems bridge the gap between the ineffable and the human. Her writing is clear and pure and the poems are exquisitely executed. This collection will bring comfort to those with a religion of their own, as well as those seeking a relationship with some kind of higher power."
—Satya Robyn, author of *The Most Beautiful Thing* and *Thaw*

Without Ceasing

The wash of dawn across the sky
reveals Your signature.

Cicadas drone Your praise
through the honey-slow afternoon.

The angular windmills on the ridge
recite Your name with every turn.

And I, who can barely focus on breath
without drifting into story:

what can I say to You,
author of wisteria and sorrel,

You who shaped these soft hills
with glaciers' slow passage?

You fashioned me as a gong:
your presence reverberates.

Help me to open my lips
that I may sing Your praise.

Winter Psalm

The wind whips spirals of snow
dervishes dancing across icy asphalt

snowplows call out to one another
backing up to ply their routes again

the atmosphere looms, pregnant
with the promise of precipitation

and I? I scatter handfuls of cat litter
across the driveway's uneven terrain

casting prayers for the safe passage
of all who come, and all who go

Rachel Barenblat

Prayer Before Building the Sukkah

for the sturdiness of my house
and for the willingness to leave it

for this chance to build
a temporary home, to remember

nomad desert wandering
and harvest houses: thank You.

Connect me, God, with all who labor
here and everywhere.

Increase my compassion
for anyone who has no home.

There is no Temple, and I do not farm:
all I can offer You

is the work of my hands
my heart, open as these walls.

The House
at the Center
of the World

Poetic Midrash on Sacred Space

Abe Mezrich

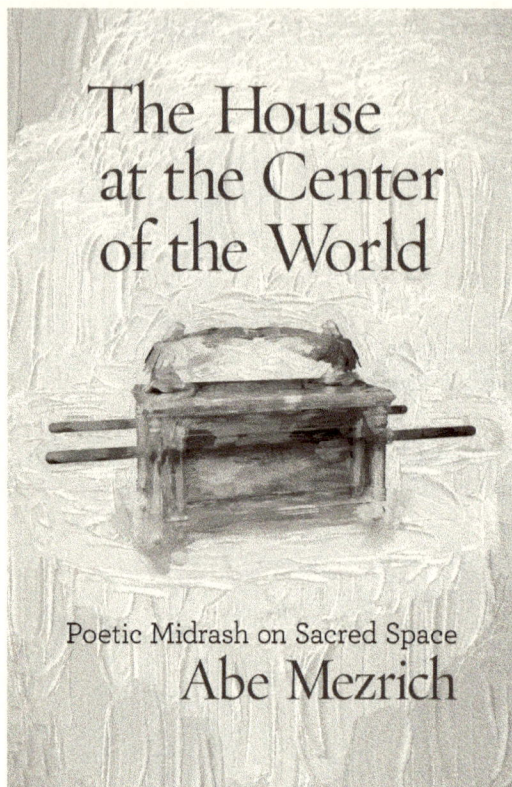

"Each installment of Abe's still small voice is a miniature jewel, poetically illuminating with its delicate facets otherwise hidden elements of each parsha.

Dan Friedman, managing editor, The Forward

Abe Mezrich cuts straight back to the roots of the Midrashic tradition, sermonizing as a poet, rather than idealogue. He can quickly build up sacred spaces in the manner of Eastern haiku-writers, or rhythmically zoom through ideas with tight free verse cadences, familiar to American readers. Best of all, Abe knows how to ask questions and avoid the obvious answers.

Jake Marmer, poet and performer

These poems remind us that our Creator is forgiving, that the spiritual and physical can inform one another, and that the supernatural can be carried into the everyday.

Yehoshua November, author of *God's Optimism*

Abe Mezrich

Spirituality

God speaks

from between the two cherubim

sculpted onto the Ark-cover

that rests on the wooden Ark

where the recorded Law

—the list of rules—

is kept.

*

The plain,

the basic

upholds the mystical.

Exodus 25:10-22

You Come to God for Yourself

i
How is the Golden Calf made?
The people take *the gold rings of* their *wives,* their *sons,* their *daughters.*
Aaron takes the rings and casts them into a fire.
And the Golden Calf comes of this.

ii
How is God's Tent made?
God says: let *every person whose heart so moves him* offer gold and
silver and copper and cloth and jewels.
And every man must pay a *half-shekel…for his soul.*
These half-shekels will fund the work of the *Mishkan.*

*

To make the Golden Calf, you hand over your wife's jewelry, your
children's jewelry--someone else's jewelry.
To make God's house, you give of your own *heart,* of your own *soul.*

iii
You can come to the Divine yourself.
Or you can expect that others will come to the Divine for you.
*

Which of these options you choose
is the difference between the path to idol-worship
and the path toward the house of God.

Exodus 32:1-6; 25:2; 30:11-16

Abe Mezrich

Why we pray in groups

i

The Torah speaks twice of the completion of the building of God's
Tent.

*

In the first telling
(at the close of the Book of Exodus)
God comes to the Tent
and Moses cannot enter—
because who can come before God?
But then God calls to Moses
and speaks to him.

*

In the second telling (in the Book of Numbers)
the Princes of the Tribes of Israel
volunteer gifts,
donations for the Tent from each tribe.
And following the Princes' gift-giving
Moses walks into the Tent,
and God speaks to Moses.

ii

Alone, you wait for God's grace.
But the entire people can march up to God's Tent.
Following the people,
you can come to the place of God,
to the place where God speaks to you.

Exodus 40:35, Numbers Chapter 7

from the **Coffee House** of **Jewish Dreamers**

Poems of *Wonder and Wandering*

Isidore Century

"So rich, so full of life,
so much *ta'am*, tastiness."
– *Home Planet News*

"FROM THE COFFEE HOUSE OF JEWISH DREAMERS is so rich, so full of life, and has so much *ta'am*, tastiness, that it is almost daunting to review.
—**Nikki Stiller,** *Home Planet News*

"Isidore Century is a wonderful poet. He writes of traveling to Coney Island; visiting Israel and returning there to the land of Yiddish in which he grew up; his father, who escaped from Poland and made his way illegally to the U.S., where he became an official in the Painter's Union; and about his own reluctant and penetrating faith, 'I keep running from a God/in whom I do not believe/hoping he catches me.'

"His poems are brief stories: they're funny, deeply observed, without pretension, written with a knowingness and rhythm of things old and new. Those related to Torah readings are poetic, original midrashim. He brings the figures of the Bible to Central Park, or places the poet in Egypt and service as Joseph's valet and butler, adding his distinctive accent to the text."
—*The New York Jewish Week*

My Father's Hands

even now,
knowing my skin
knowing my skin is raw
from his untouchings,
knowing his hands were frozen
by his father's untouchings,
knowing a gravestone
stands between us
like a wall between his room and mine

even now,
his calloused hands
reach towards me
from a graveyard of lost childhoods
asking
for my hands.

I Embrace

I embrace the wild and mad dogs within me.
I embrace the yellow-eyed tiger
      raging through the underbrush of my smiles.
I embrace the befouler
      savagely trained into vanity
      and I embrace vanity also.
I embrace the outcast sibling
      howling in the distant hills beyond reason.
I embrace the shapeless monsters of the night
I have feared
I have hidden
I have been.
I embrace all manner of beast
      that I am.

Isidore Century

Moses (4)

He couldn't swim.
He was afraid of water.
So were 600,000 former slaves.
And there was the Red Sea!
And there were Pharaoh's chariots!
"Go in," God said. " The water's fine."
He went in,
up to his ankles,
up to his knees,
up to his nose...
He took a faithful step;
the waters parted !
The people followed him onto dry land.
Behind them, "horse and rider He hurled into the sea."
On the way to the Promised Land.
in the pool at each oasis,
a few non-*yeshiva buchers* taught themselves to swim,
just in case they came to another Red Sea.
"You have to hope for miracles," they said,
   "but cannot rely on them."

(and it came to pass
many generations later,
one of their grandchildren, Marc Spitz,
became an Olympic swimming champion of champions.)

From the Coffee House of Jewish Dreamers

About the author

A community organizer by training, born and bred in New York, Sue Swartz now lives contentedly in Bloomington, Indiana where she writes, makes art, builds Jewish community, and obsesses about how the world is going to hell in a hand basket. Her poetry in conversation with Biblical text has been published in numerous journals and anthologies and was nominated for a Pushcart Prize. She often changes her mind in the middle of things and wishes she was taller.

www.ingramcontent.com/pod-product-compliance
Lightning Source LLC
Chambersburg PA
CBHW021404090426
42742CB00009B/998